ALLERGIES

ALLERGIES

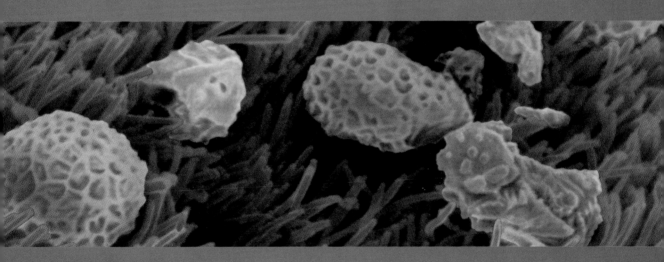

Terry Allan Hicks

Marshall Cavendish
Benchmark
New York

With thanks to the Ursos and Dr. Matczuk.

Marshall Cavendish Benchmark
99 White Plains Road
Tarrytown, New York 10591-9001
www.marshallcavendish.us

This book is not intended for use as a substitute for advice, consultation, or treatment by a licensed medical practitioner. The reader is advised that no action of a medical nature should be taken without consultation with a licensed medical practitioner, including action that may seem to be indicated by the contents of this work, since individual circumstances vary and medical standards, knowledge, and practices change with time. The publisher, author, and medical consultants disclaim all liability and cannot be held responsible for any problems that may arise from use of this book.

Library of Congress Cataloging-in-Publication Data

Hicks, Terry Allan.
  Allergies / by Terry Allan Hicks.
      p. cm. — (Health alert)
  Summary: "Discusses allergies and their effects on people and
society"—Provided by publisher.
  Includes index.
  ISBN 0-7614-1918-7
  1. Allergy—Juvenile literature. I. Title. II. Series: Health alert
(Benchmark Books)

  RC585.H53 2005
  616.97—dc22

2005005000

Front cover: Different types of pollen
Title page: Allergens in the trachea

Photo research by Candlepants Incorporated
Front cover: Science Photo Library/Photo Researchers, Inc. / David Scharf
The photographs in this book are used by permission and through the courtesy of: *Photo Researchers, Inc.:* D. Lovegrove, 11; Stem Jems, 13, 15; E. Gray, 14; Gilbert S. Grant, 17; Astrid & Hanns-Frieder Michler, 18; Ralph C. Eagle Jr., 20; John Kaprielian, 24, 31; Scott Camazine, 25 (left), 25 (right); Mark Clarke, 51; AJPhoto, 55; Susan Leavines, 56. *Science Photo Library / Photo Researchers, Inc.:* 34; Mark Clarke, 19; Paul Rapson, 41; Saturn Stills, 42; Mark Thomas, 44, 57; Andrew Syred, 47; John Bavosi, 53. *Corbis:* Royalty Free, 23; Ariel Skelley, 28; Bettmann, 33; Hulton-Deutsch Collection, 36; Jose Luis Pelaez, Inc., 39. *Visuals Unlimited:* Brad Morgen, 45. *Getty Creative:* Photodisc Green, 49.

Printed in China
6 5 4 3 2 1

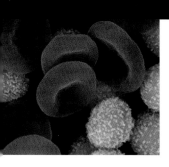

CONTENTS

1

WHAT IS IT LIKE TO HAVE ALLERGIES?

When she felt the bee sting her foot, Stephanie did not think much about it. "I had been stung before—at least nine times," the Connecticut fifth-grader says, "and nothing bad ever happened." So she just reached down and squashed the bee. Then she and her family went back to enjoying a lazy Sunday afternoon riding jet skis on a lake in Vermont.

But *this* bee sting was different from all the others. A minute or two after she was stung, Stephanie's face began to break out in red itchy patches, called **hives.** That was when her mother, Jeanne, realized she must be allergic to bee stings.

"I guess I am the nervous type of mom," Jeanne says. "That is why I always carry medication with me, including allergy medication. So when I saw the hives starting to appear on Stephanie's face, I gave her a spoonful of the medication right away."

Even after she took the medication, Stephanie's symptoms became worse—much worse. "My lips were getting numb," she remembers, "and they felt all tingly." The hives were spreading all over her body. And her foot was now badly swollen where the bee had stung it.

Jeanne knew she had to get her daughter to a doctor right away. But that was not going to be easy. Stephanie and her family were on vacation, and they did not know the area well. By the time they reached the shore of the lake, Stephanie was beginning to get sleepy—a **side effect** of the medication she had taken. The numbness was spreading across her face. Worst of all, she was beginning to have trouble breathing.

Stephanie's family could not find a doctor's office that was open on a Sunday afternoon, so they rushed to a nearby police station. Stephanie took another dose of the medication while the police called an ambulance. It was another twenty-five minutes before Stephanie reached a nearby hospital and received the medical treatment she needed.

The doctors at the hospital confirmed what Jeanne had suspected: Stephanie had a severe allergic reaction to bee venom—the **toxin** that the bee had injected into her body when it stung her. And they told her that if she had not had the medication handy, Stephanie might have died.

When Stephanie's family returned to their home, Stephanie went to see Dr. Agnes Matczuk, an **allergist**—a doctor who specializes in allergies. Dr. Matczuk gave her a series of allergy tests, exposing her to small amounts of different substances that can cause allergies. The results showed that Stephanie was allergic to five different types of stinging insects, including bees, hornets, and wasps.

"Most of the allergies I see are not as serious as Stephanie's," Dr. Matczuk says. "But perhaps 10 percent of the allergies to stinging insects that I see fall into the severe category. And, of course, they are much more of a problem in the summertime, when insects are especially active."

Dr. Matczuk recommended a course of **immunotherapy**— sometimes called "allergy shots"—for Stephanie. "Whether [a patient has] immunotherapy depends on many factors," she says. "If an allergy is mild, or seasonal—for example, a sensitivity to grass **pollen**—it may be better just to treat the **symptoms** for a few months out of the year. But in a severe case like Stephanie's, immunotherapy is usually the best approach to take."

Stephanie now visits Dr. Matczuk regularly, to receive injections with small doses of bee venom. It is not much fun.

"I hate getting shots," she admits—but it should help to reduce her allergic sensitivity to bee venom, in case she is stung again.

If she *is* stung again, Stephanie will be ready. She now carries a special medication that fights severe allergic reactions. If she develops an allergic reaction to something, she can use the medication immediately.

Stephanie has also learned to change her behavior in ways that will reduce her chances of being stung. "I cannot wear bright-colored clothes anymore, or flowered dresses," she says. "And I am not supposed to wear perfume or anything like that. It all attracts bees."

Even though she is still scared whenever she sees a bee, Stephanie is determined not to let her allergies keep her from doing the things she loves to do, such as sports and other outdoor activities.

2

WHAT ARE ALLERGIES?

In the United States, almost one person in five suffers from allergies. For many of these people, their allergic symptoms are not much more than an annoyance. Millions of people live with the sniffling and sneezing of **hay fever,** for example. But for others, allergies can be life-threatening—and life-changing.

Most allergic reactions are quite mild, and are concentrated in the part of the body that has come into contact with an **allergen**, which is a foreign substance that has entered the body. Bee venom, pollen, and dust are types of allergens. For example, someone who has accidentally brushed a patch of poison ivy with his or her hand may experience a painful **rash** and itching on that hand, but nowhere else.

A moderate reaction extends beyond the part of the body where the allergen is found. In the case of a poison ivy allergy, this could include rashes or itching in other parts of the body far away from the hand. A moderate allergic reaction might even involve breathing difficulties.

In a severe allergic reaction, the symptoms spread throughout the entire body. This may begin simply, with mild symptoms such as itching or a rash around the face. But within minutes, there may be swelling in different parts of the body, including the throat—which makes

Allergies—and the problems and reactions they cause—affect millions of Americans every year.

swallowing and breathing difficult. Other symptoms of a severe reaction can include vomiting, stomach cramps, or diarrhea. A person having the reaction may also become dizzy and confused.

This type of extreme allergic reaction is called **anaphylaxis** or anaphylactic shock. In the most severe cases, it can cause death. The most common causes of anaphylaxis are allergies to food (especially peanuts), penicillin (a type of medication), and bee venom. More than 200 people die every year in the United States from anaphylaxis caused by food allergies. Most of them are children.

But most allergies are not as dangerous as this. For many people, an allergy may mean nothing more than a stuffy nose, or a patch of red, itchy skin. But even mild allergies are a real problem for the people who have them. And allergies are a huge problem for society as a whole.

WHAT CAUSES ALLERGIES?

An allergy is an extreme sensitivity to the presence of allergens in the body. Allergens may enter the body when we breathe, when we eat, or when we touch something. An allergic reaction is a result of what happens in the body when a person is exposed to an allergen.

The human body must protect itself against many harmful foreign substances. It does this through a very complicated set of defenses known as the **immune system.**

The immune system is designed to recognize the presence of substances, called **antigens,** that are not normally found in the body. (Allergens are types of antigens.) Other antigens may be **bacteria** or **viruses**. They may be toxins or they may even be blood or tissue from another human being (from a blood transfusion or an organ transplant).

When the immune system realizes that an antigen is present in a particular part of the body, it rushes special blood cells to that area. Some of these blood cells actually "eat" the unwanted invader. Others attach themselves to the antigens, "marking" them so that other types of blood cells can attack them. One of these special blood cells that marks antigens is called a B-cell. It produces a special type of defense called an **antibody** or immunoglobulin.

This photograph, taken using a very strong microscope, shows the different types of blood cells. The red cells carry oxygen. The white cells help fight disease.

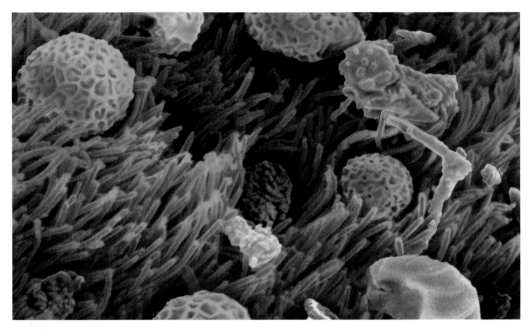

Allergens such as dust and pollen collect on microscopic hairs of the trachea. The trachea—sometimes called the windpipe—is an important part of the respiratory system.

There are five types of antibodies: IgA, IgD, IgE, IgG, and IgM. They are very effective in fighting infections and other health problems. But one of them, the IgE antibody, sometimes overreacts to the presence of an antigen—and this is where an allergy begins.

The Stages of an Allergic Reaction

The first stage of an allergic reaction is known as sensitization. An allergen enters the body, and the immune system responds by creating various types of antibodies. In a person with a normal immune system, this is not usually a problem. But in a person who has allergies, the body creates an unusually large number of IgE antibodies.

There are no symptoms during the sensitization stage. There may not be any symptoms for days, weeks, months, or even years. But this does not mean that nothing is happening inside the body.

During this time, the IgE antibodies are attaching themselves to special blood cells called mast cells. Mast cells are found almost everywhere in the body, but they concentrate in two places: blood vessels and epithelium. Epithelium is the thin layer of cells that covers the parts of the body that come into contact with the outside world—in the nose and throat, for example. These are also places where allergens are likely to be found.

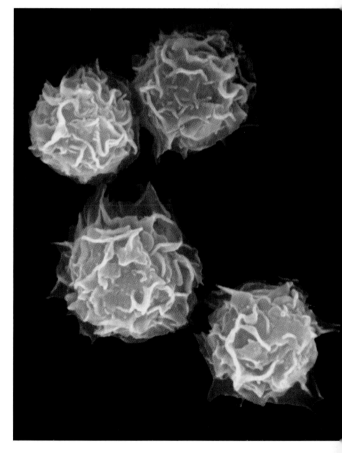

Mast cells in the blood (shown here) release chemicals when an allergen touches them. These chemicals cause allergic reactions.

The next stage of an allergic reaction is called activation. This happens when the body is exposed again to the allergen that has caused it to create a large number of IgE antibodies. But activation does not necessarily occur the second time the allergen enters the body. In fact, it is possible that the body can be exposed to the same allergen hundreds of times, before a person develops symptoms. During this time, the mast cells—loaded with IgE antibodies—are waiting.

When activation finally occurs, the mast cells begin to release several different kinds of chemicals that cause allergy symptoms. One of these chemicals, called **histamine,** makes the cells of the epithelium produce a watery—sometimes sticky—fluid called mucus. This is why allergic reactions often cause a stuffed-up or runny nose.

Histamine also causes swelling and **inflammation** in many of the areas it affects. Swollen tissues in the throat and other parts of the respiratory system (the organs you use to breathe) can make breathing very difficult. Muscles that help with the breathing process may also be affected by an allergic reaction.

Blood vessels around the body can be affected by an allergic reaction. When this happens, fluid begins to leak from blood vessels. Tissues in the body start to become

Sources of Allergies

One of the reasons allergies are so common is that the substances that cause them are everywhere.

The Air We Breathe
The air may look perfectly clear, but it is actually filled with millions of tiny particles of dust, **dust mites, mold, dander,** and—especially during the spring, summer, and fall—pollen. All these things can cause allergic reactions when they are breathed in.

The Food We Eat
Many people are allergic to common foods, including peanut butter, milk, eggs, and fish. Food allergies are probably the most common—and the most dangerous—of all allergies, especially for children.

Poison sumac

The Medication We Take
Doctors who prescribe certain drugs must watch carefully for signs of allergic reactions. Most people can take these medications without any trouble at all. But for a few patients, allergies may cause symptoms ranging from a skin rash (also called dermatitis) to breathing difficulties or even death.

The Products We Buy
The stores we shop in are full of products that contain allergens. Cosmetics, such as makeup, perfume, and soap, can cause allergic reactions. Many people are highly allergic to **latex,** the main ingredient in everything from car tires to kitchen gloves. And others cannot touch certain types of metal—especially nickel, which is often used in car parts and jewelry—without breaking out in a rash.

The Plants and Animals around Us
Doctors estimate that more than two million people in the United States are allergic to the stings of bees or other insect. And at least 70 percent of Americans have allergies to poison ivy, posion sumac, and other wild plants that grow all over the country.

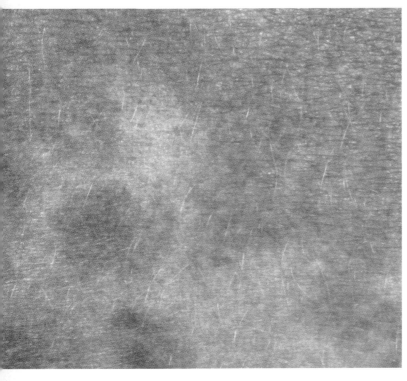

Allergies often cause skin rashes, like the one shown here, which was caused by a food allergy.

swollen, often causing itchy or hot rashes and hives on the skin.

The intestines—a part of the digestive system—can be affected by allergies. As a result, some people with allergic reactions suffer from stomach pain or problems going to the bathroom.

Symptoms of allergic reactions usually go away once the allergen is out of a person's immune system and when the person is no longer exposed to the allergen. Medication is also often given to help ease the discomfort caused by these symptoms. Medication, however, cannot destroy the allergens in the body—the immune system must do its job and destroy the allergens.

TYPES OF ALLERGIC CONDITIONS

Allergic reactions affect an allergy sufferer in many different and complicated ways. Different types of allergies affect various parts of the body, causing a variety of different symptoms.

Sneezing is the body's way to relieve irritation in the airways. Sometimes this irritation is caused by dust, pollen, or other small particles that have entered the nose.

Allergic Rhinitis

For millions of people, the symptoms of allergic rhinitis are all too familiar: watery eyes, sneezing, a nose that is either runny or stuffed up ("rhinitis" is Latin for "swollen nose"), and a scratchy feeling in the mouth, nose, and throat. This condition is known as hay fever, even though it really has nothing to do with hay and does not cause a fever.

Allergic rhinitis is by far the most common allergic reaction. It is often caused by microscopic particles of pollen floating through the air. Many different plants produce pollen. But the most serious allergen-producing plants are grasses, weeds, and trees.

19

This is a magnified view of pollen grains from a ragweed plant. The pollen's spiky outside help it stick to plants, insects, and, unfortunately, people.

Pollen particles are usually tiny—sometimes smaller than the width of a human hair—so they are easy to breathe in. And plants spread them in huge amounts, especially at certain times of the year. During pollen season, you may inhale hundreds of pollen particles with every breath.

The allergy season varies widely, depending on which allergens a person is allergic to. Trees usually produce pollen in the spring, while the pollen season for grasses spreads across spring and early summer. Ragweed plants—which by themselves probably cause most Americans' allergic symptoms—pollinates in summer and early fall.

But not all airborne (in the air) allergens are seasonal. Many are found indoors, where the changing seasons may have little or no effect on them. These allergens include dust, mold, animal dander, dust mites, and even dried-up bits of dead cockroaches and other insects. All of these things can float through the air and be breathed in. And all of them can cause allergies.

Asthma

Asthma is one of the most serious allergy-related conditions. It is a disease of the respiratory system that causes the airways leading to the lungs to become tighter and narrower, making it very difficult to breathe. The symptoms of asthma include wheezing (making a squeaky or whistling sound while breathing), coughing, and a feeling of tightness in the chest. A severe asthma attack can cause death, if it is not treated quickly enough.

In recent years, asthma has become more and more common. As many as 17 million people in the United States may suffer from this condition. Researchers believe that about 60 percent of all cases of asthma (and 90 percent in children) are caused by allergies.

Many of the same allergens that cause allergic rhinitis also cause asthma, including pollen, animal dander, dust, and mold. But asthma can also be triggered by allergies to food, drugs, cosmetics products, or cigarette smoke.

Drug Allergies

Many commonly used medications can cause allergic reactions. A drug allergy may result in a skin rash, itching of the skin or eyes, and sometimes swelling of the nose or throat. In more severe cases, the reactions could include a bluish tint to the skin, nausea, vomiting, breathing difficulties, and anaphylaxis. Some researchers believe that 75 percent of fatal (deadly) anaphylactic reactions result from penicillin allergies. Penicillin is a commonly used **antibiotic.**

Food Allergies

Food allergies are very common in children, and especially babies. These allergies often disappear as the child gets older. Around 90 percent of children's food allergies are caused by just six types of food: wheat, eggs, milk, soy, tree nuts (such as walnuts and almonds), and peanuts. Most adults' food allergies are caused by fish (especially shellfish such as shrimps, crabs, and lobsters), peanuts, or tree nuts.

The symptoms of a food allergy include a "tingling" feeling in the mouth, followed by a swollen tongue and throat. Then a rash or hives may appear, on the face or elsewhere. (A skin condition called **eczema** is a common

Many people around the world are allergic to shellfish such as lobsters, crabs, and shrimp.

reaction to a food allergy among small children.) In severe cases, these symptoms may be followed by vomiting, breathing difficulties, or anaphylaxis.

Plant Allergies

Three wild plants that grow all over North America—poison ivy, poison oak, and poison sumac—contain an oily allergen called urushiol. When an allergic person touches the plant, a red, painfully itchy rash will appear. The rash often occurs

The poison ivy plant grows wild throughout the United States. You should always be careful about what plant you touch—it could be poison ivy, poison oak, or poison sumac. An allergic reaction to the plant's oils is a very unpleasant experience.

where the plant touched the skin. The rash then turns into blisters, which are fluid-filled bumps. These symptoms are very unpleasant, but usually not very serious. However, urushiol can be very dangerous if it is inhaled. For example, if someone throws some poison ivy on a fire and then inhales the smoke, he or she may come down with a very bad rash, a fever, or a lung infection.

Insect Stings

The insects that are most likely to cause allergic reactions are bees, wasps, yellowjackets, hornets, and fire ants. All of them have stingers that inject venom into their victims. Most people will have a reaction to an insect sting, with pain, redness, and swelling around the immediate area of the sting. But a person who is allergic to these stings will have a much more serious reaction. The symptoms can range from rashes and swelling in areas far away from the sting, all the way to breathing difficulties, vomiting, diarrhea, anaphylaxis, and sometimes even death.

 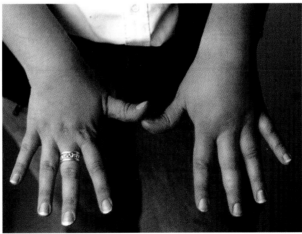

A bee injects venom through the stinger on its abdomen. The venom can cause a painful allergic reaction, like the swollen left hand above.

Multiple Chemical Sensitivity

In recent years, medical researchers have noticed an increase in a condition known as multiple chemical sensitivity (MCS) or environmental illness. People who suffer from MCS report a wide range of symptoms, from headache and sneezing to extreme tiredness and depression.

Some of these people and their doctors believe that their condition is a kind of "multiple allergy," caused by exposure to many different chemicals found in the environment today. They point to cosmetics, paints, and pollution as possible triggers for their symptoms. But many medical experts do not believe that MCS is a real condition, and think that some other cause is to blame.

Cosmetic Allergies

The cosmetic products that many people use, such as perfumes, soaps, shampoos, and makeup—can cause allergic reactions. Cosmetic allergies are quite common, but are not usually very serious. Typical symptoms are skin rash, itching, and swelling—usually in the area where the cosmetics are used. A cosmetic allergy may take weeks, months, or even years of exposure before it appears.

Latex Allergy

Latex, which is made from the sap of the rubber tree, is used in all kinds of products, including tires and house paint. People with this condition may react to the touch of rubber. They may develop itchiness and rashes, chest pain, difficulty breathing, and even anaphylactic shock. Some studies suggest that as many as 10 percent of all health care workers, who often wear special latex gloves to protect themselves and their patients from infection, are allergic to latex. Many of these people use non-latex gloves, but some doctors and nurses have actually had to quit medicine and take up another line of work because they could not even touch surgical gloves.

Allergic Conjunctivitis

This condition is common in children and affects the eyes. Conjunctivitis means inflammation of the conjunctiva, which is a part of the eye. Its symptoms include red, itchy, watery eyes, and sometimes blurred vision. The causes of conjunctivitis include allergies to pollen, animal dander, cosmetics, and cigarette smoke.

WHO GETS ALLERGIES?

Perhaps the most puzzling question about allergies is this: Why do some people react to common substances, while others do not? Medical researchers do not really know yet, but they do know that heredity is an important factor. Heredity is the passing on of characteristics or traits from a parent to a child. For example, you might inherit your parent's hair color or eye color.

Allergies can be passed down from parent to child. But just because your parents have allergies does not necessarily mean you will have them too.

If one of a child's parents has an allergy, there is about a 30 percent chance that the child will, too. If both parents suffer from allergies, the odds go up to at least 75 percent. But this does not mean that the child will have the *same* allergies. Some—such as a sensitivity to shellfish—are commonly passed on, but others are not. Researchers believe that a parent can pass on a tendency to have allergies even if the parent does not actually suffer from an allergy.

Another factor that helps to determine who gets allergies is the environment. Old houses and apartment buildings often have large amounts of allergy-causing dust, mold, and insects. And many office buildings today are "sealed," with heating and air-conditioning systems that trap air and allergens inside. People who live and work in these buildings are probably more likely to develop allergies.

Allergies seem to be more common today than in the past. One reason may be that patients and doctors are now much more knowledgeable about allergies. So people are more likely to recognize an allergic reaction, and their doctors are more likely to identify and treat it correctly.

Another factor contributing to the increase in allergies may be the growing use of antibiotics to fight infections. Some studies suggest that antibiotics—especially when given to children—may change the immune system's response to antigens.

Changes in people's lifestyles are definitely making a difference, too. In the past, people who lived far from the ocean would rarely have eaten shellfish, for example. But today, lobsters and other crustaceans that come from places like Maine are delivered all over the world. So people everywhere can enjoy these foods—and maybe develop allergies to them.

3

THE HISTORY OF ALLERGIES

Allergies may be more common today, but they have been around for a very long time. According to carvings on his tomb, the Egyptian pharaoh Menes died in about 2640 B.C.E. from what was probably an allergic reaction to a wasp's sting.

More than two thousand years ago, Hebrew and Greek doctors described the symptoms of both allergies and asthma. And the ancient Roman writer Lucretius was probably talking about allergies when he wrote a saying we still use today: "One man's meat is another man's . . . poison."

By the sixteenth century, doctors were able to diagnose allergies and asthma, and sometimes to treat them successfully. In 1552, an Italian doctor offered an asthma cure that would be familiar to patients today: eat right, get plenty of rest and exercise, and sleep on a bed with no feathers in it.

Other doctors of the time wrote descriptions of allergies, and made the connection between allergens—including flowers and cat hair—and allergy symptoms. But it was not until 1656 that the first scientific allergy tests were conducted. A French doctor, Pierre Borel, thought one of his patients might be allergic to eggs, so he placed some material from an egg on the man's skin. Blisters soon appeared on the man's skin.

In the 1870s, a British doctor named Charles Blackley was the first doctor to identify the cause of hay fever. He suffered from it himself, and he thought grass pollen—not hay, as farmers had always believed—might be the reason. He saved

Early scientists made the connection between allergies and flowering plants and grasses. Today we know that plants, like common ragweed, cause hay fever and other allergic reactions.

some pollen in a jar until winter, when all the grass was dead. Then he opened the jar, breathed in the pollen—and immediately began sneezing.

Blackley also proved that pollen could be carried on the wind for great distances. He sent "pollen traps" more than one thousand feet into the air, using kites. When he brought the kites down, he found traces of pollen in them.

IDENTIFYING THE ILLNESS

By the late nineteenth century, doctors had a new understanding of what caused many medical conditions. Much of their knowledge grew out of the work of a great French chemist named Louis Pasteur.

Pasteur suggested a radical new idea—that disease could be caused by tiny microorganisms entering the body, and that the body could produce its own defenses against it. Pasteur created the new science of immunology (the study of the immune system). Much of the research into allergies that followed was built on his work.

In 1901, two scientists in Paris, Paul Portier and Charles Richet, began studying the stings of several sea animals that produce toxins. They extracted toxin from sea anemones, then gave very small amounts of it—amounts that should not have been harmful—to a test animal. The results were very puzzling.

The first two doses of toxin did not seem to bother the test animal at all—but the third dose killed it. Portier and Richet decided that the animal's death must have been caused by the body's response to repeated exposure to the toxin. They invented a new word for this effect: *anaphylaxis,* which means "the opposite of protection."

At about the same time, two other scientists—Emil von Behring in Germany and Shibasaburo Kitasato in Japan—were studying the effects of a different type of substance. This substance, called an antitoxin, was produced by the bodies of people and animals who were suffering from an extremely dangerous disease called diphtheria.

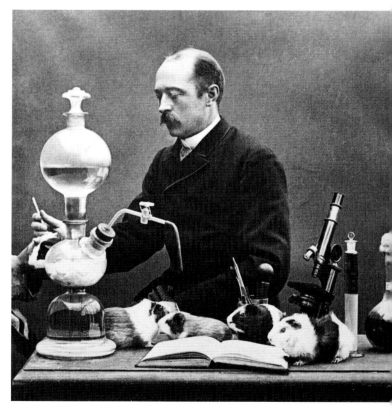

Emil von Behring won the Nobel Prize for his research on antitoxins that can create immunity to disease.

The bacteriologist Shibasaburo Kitasato worked with von Behring in Germany, before opening a research institute in his native Japan.

The scientists found that small amounts of this antitoxin would keep animals from becoming sick if they were later exposed to the bacteria that cause diphtheria. They thought that this could be an effective treatment against the disease, but it had a very strange side effect on the person taking the antitoxin.

Some of the people who were given the antitoxin became sick, and some of them even died. This was very hard to understand, because the antitoxin was not actually poisonous. It should not have harmed anyone, but it did.

Von Behring and Kitasato noticed that people and animals were more likely to become sick if they were given the antitoxin more than once. Scientists were fascinated by this tendency. In 1906, Clemens von Pirquet of Austria, gave this tendency the name *Allergie.* It is a German term he created by combining the Greek words *allos* and *ergon,* which together mean "altered reaction."

Within the next few years, other researchers had shown that allergies were connected to some of the most common respiratory problems, including asthma and hay fever. And Henry Dale, a British scientist, discovered the chemical that came to be called histamine.

ALLERGY TREATMENTS

Doctors were also looking for new ways to treat allergies. In 1911, Leonard Noon of Britain gave the first allergy shots. These were injections of material taken from grass pollen. He thought this might be an effective treatment for hay fever. It was not, but it laid the groundwork for future developments in immunotherapy.

By the 1920s, doctors were beginning to specialize in treating allergies. Two of these "allergists," Robert Coca and Arthur Cooke of the United States, showed that some allergies, including hay fever and asthma, could be passed on from parents to their children.

In the 1930s, researchers took important steps based on Henry Dale's discovery of histamine. Wilhelm Feldberg of Germany and his American colleague Carl Draystedt found that the body produces histamine during anaphylaxis. In 1937, a Swiss scientist, Daniel Bovet, created the first *anti*histamine—a drug to fight the effects of histamine.

It had been known since the early 1920s that antibodies produced by the immune system caused allergic reactions. But it was not until 1967 that Kimishige and Teruko Ishizaka, a husband-and-wife team in Japan, proved which antibody was responsible, when they identified the IgE antibody.

The basic treatments for allergies have not changed greatly

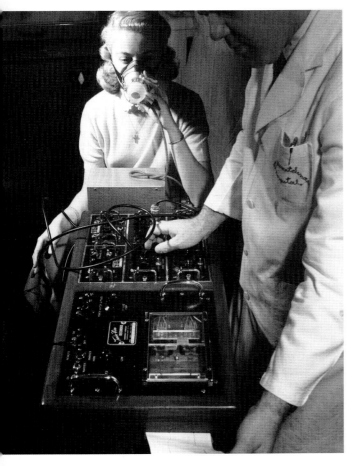

This photograph, taken around the late 1950s, shows a woman participating in allergy research. Here, a researcher uses a machine to measure her breathing.

for decades. But as the twenty-first century begins, researchers are looking at very different ways of dealing with allergies and their symptoms.

One of the most interesting is an antibody that actually fights the IgE antibody. Scientists created this "anti-antibody" by injecting laboratory animals with IgE, then removing the antibodies the animals produced and making them into a medication. Tests show that this treatment can greatly reduce the number of IgE antibodies in the blood.

Much of today's allergy research focuses on **genetics** and heredity. These researchers are trying to understand why some allergies are passed on from parents to their children. Researchers have discovered at least one gene (a group of molecules that holds the basic genetic information about a human being) that causes a tendency toward having allergies. And others believe they have discovered the genetic coding that tells the body how much of the IgE antibody to produce.

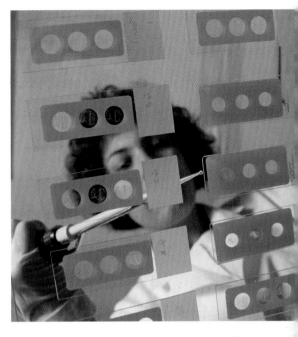

Allergy research continues today and will continue into the future. Perhaps someday a cure can be found.

Someday, this genetic research may result in more effective treatments for allergies. Some scientists believe that an allergy sufferer's genes could be altered. This might prevent IgE antibodies from attaching themselves to mast cells. This could even stop the body from producing so many IgE antibodies.

All of these areas of research show great promise. But it will probably be many years before any of them actually result in an allergy treatment that can be used in the real world. For now, most allergy sufferers will have to rely on the same treatments that have been used for decades.

4

LIVING WITH ALLERGIES

Many people do not even know that they suffer from allergies. The symptoms of hay fever are easy to mistake for those of the common cold. And someone might not suspect that a rash on the face or hands is the result of an allergy to penicillin, or peanut butter, or perfume.

It is possible to go a long time without seeking real medical treatment for allergies, especially for mild ones that are not recognized as allergies. Some people just ignore the symptoms, and hope they will go away on their own. Sometimes the symptoms do. Others treat the symptoms with over-the-counter drugs (medication that can be bought without a prescription) such as decongestants.

In some cases, however, people begin to realize that their symptoms are not a sign of a different illness. Someone who thinks she just has a lot of colds may notice that these "colds" tend to appear during certain seasons. At this point, many people will seek the help of an allergist.

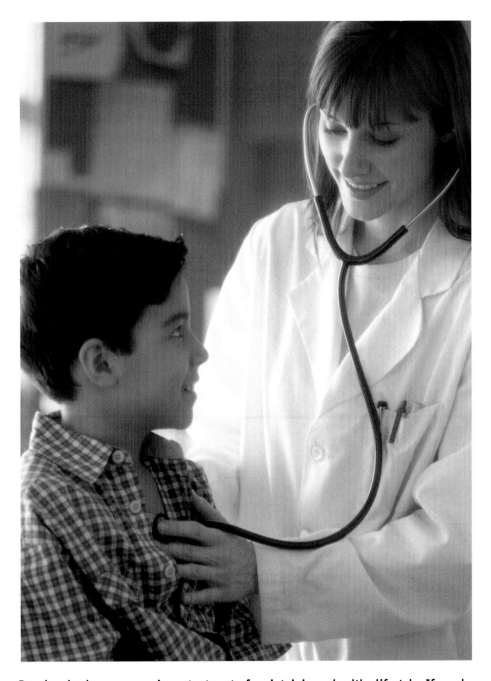

Regular check-ups are an important part of maintaining a healthy lifestyle. If you have allergies, your family doctor might send you to an allergist for treatment.

DIAGNOSING ALLERGIES

The first step an allergist takes in diagnosing—or identifying—a patient's problems will usually be to ask a lot of questions. Some of the most important questions will concern the patient's family history. The allergist will want to know whether anyone else in the house suffers from allergies, and if so, what kinds.

The allergist will want to know what the patient's symptoms are, and when and where they occur. Do the symptoms appear all the time, or just during certain seasons? And do they happen everywhere, or just in certain places?

Other important question will concern the patient's environment. Are there pets in the house? Does the patient live in an older building, where there might be mold, or sleep in a bed with a feather pillow or feather bedding?

Then the doctor will perform a physical examination, looking for telltale signs of allergies, such as swelling in the nose and throat or rashes. The doctor may also order blood tests to rule out medical conditions other than allergies—infections, for example—that could be causing the symptoms. Another possibility is a breathing test, to check for asthma. In this type of test, the patient breathes into a machine that measures lung capacity, or how much air can be held in the lungs. If the lung capacity is very low, it may be a sign that the patient has asthma. But medical science now has a number of useful tests available to determine whether a patient is truly allergic.

Skin Prick Test

This is the most common, and usually the most effective, test for allergies. It is also very simple: The doctor pricks the patient's skin with a small pointed object (sometimes a needle) covered with a very small amount of an allergen. If the patient is allergic to that allergen, the skin in the area

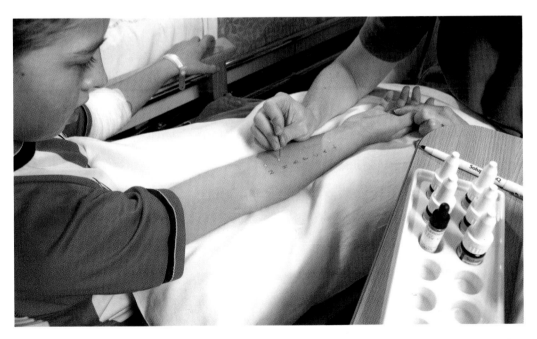

One simple way allergists test for some allergies is to prick the skin with an allergen. If the patient is allergic, the skin will quickly swell up and turn red.

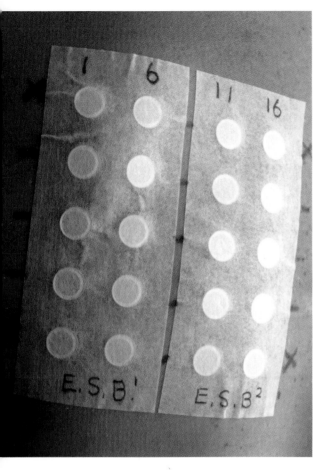

Patch tests are often performed on a person's back. The back provides the allergist with a broad and flat area for the patches.

will usually be red, swollen, and itchy within a few minutes. This type of test is very effective in identifying insect, drug, and airborne allergies, but may not work as well for food allergies.

Patch Test

The patch test is commonly used to test for skin allergies. The doctor places patches with small amounts of different allergens on an area of the patient's body, then waits for about 48 hours. When the patches are removed, any area that shows redness or swelling will indicate an allergy to that particular substance.

Food Challenge Test

When an allergist suspects a food allergy, the preferred test may be a food challenge test. The patient swallows a capsule containing an allergen one day, then one that does not contain any allergens the next day. If the patient has a reaction after taking the allergen, the doctor knows that an allergy is probably causing the problem.

Radioallergosorbent Test (RAST)

Some people cannot take allergy tests that will expose them to allergens. They include very young children, and people who are so sensitive that their reaction to the allergen might damage their health. For these people, the RAST may be the best choice. This is a laboratory test on a blood sample. It identifies specific antibodies that the patient's immune system has produced in response to a particular antigen.

PREVENTING ALLERGIC REACTIONS

In most cases, an allergist's first advice to a patient will be to avoid contact with the allergens that are responsible for his or her symptoms. Sometimes this is easy. A person who has an allergy to nickel, for example, can simply avoid wearing jewelry that might contain the metal. People who know they are allergic to poison ivy can learn to identify the plant, and be sure to wear long pants and sleeves whenever they go out in the woods.

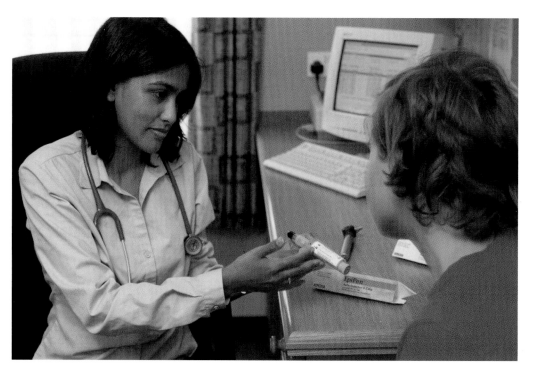

An allergist can correctly diagnose an allergy and prescribe the most effective treatment.

But it is not always possible to avoid allergens. People who are allergic to pollen cannot simply stay indoors during pollen season. Even if they did, it would not protect them completely from breathing in pollen.

However, once an allergy has been identified, it is at least a little easier to avoid the offending allergen. Food- and drug-based allergens are among the easiest to eliminate, but even that is not always easy. So what can be done to limit an allergy sufferer's exposure to allergens? That depends on the allergen.

Pollen

Most people with pollen allergies cannot avoid the millions of fine grains floating through the air. But there are some ways they can limit their exposure.

In many areas, the day's pollen count is taken by the local public health authorities, and reported in daily newspapers, on television and radio, or on the Internet. This enables allergy sufferers to stay indoors when the count is very high. They will also know to keep their windows and doors closed when there is a lot of pollen in the air.

During pollen season, allergy sufferers should use air-conditioning as much as possible, in their homes, offices, and cars.

A single plant—such as this spruce tree—may give off as many as a million particles of pollen in a single season.

They should also make sure that the conditioners' filters are cleaned regularly. Clothes should be dried indoors, not on the clothesline, so that pollen particles cannot cling to them.

Dust Mites and Mold

Even the cleanest home may have hundreds of thousands of tiny dust mites, especially on bedding and furniture. It is impossible to eliminate these allergens altogether, but there are ways of reducing exposure to them.

One way is to avoid using bedding, such as pillows and comforters, that contains feathers. The feathers can gather a lot of dust and dust mites, or the feathers themselves can be an allergen. Allergy-proof covers are available for beds and bedding. These covers prevent large amounts of dust and dust mites.

It is also very important to reduce the areas where dust can pile up. One piece of advice that allergists often give when a child has airborne allergies is to allow only one stuffed animal on the bed when he or she is sleeping. The fur on stuffed animals can gather dust, and a child can inhale a lot of this dust while sleeping.

Both dust mites and mold live best in damp conditions. Air-conditioning—which reduces the amount of moisture in

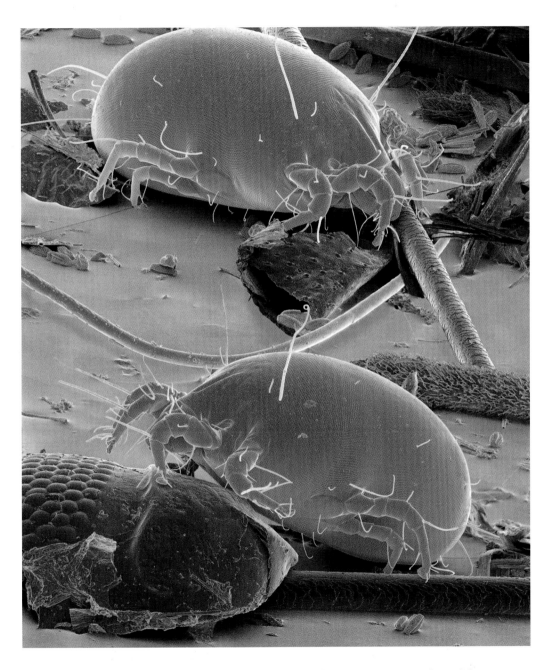

Dust mites are too small to see with the naked eye. (This picture was taken with a microscope.) Yet these tiny creatures are the second-greatest cause of allergies, after pollen.

Helpful Tips

One way to prevent allergic reactions involves washing your hair and showering. Some allergists suggest that people who are allergic to allergens like pollen should wash their hair, bathe, or take a shower at night before going to bed. By doing this, a person is able to wash out a lot of the pollen or dust that the hair and body collects during the day. This also helps to prevent your bedding from collecting a lot of allergens. For example, if you spend a lot of time outside during pollen season, you might get a lot of pollen in your hair or on your face. The pillow you rest your head on will collect a lot of these allergens. As you sleep and breathe at night, you inhale the pollen on your pillow, which can cause allergic reactions. Washing will not eliminate all allergens, but it can help to reduce them.

the air—can reduce their presence. In the winter, using a dehumidifier may help. Dehumidifiers are machines that take the moisture out of the air. But air conditioners and dehumidifiers must be cleaned regularly. Otherwise, mold can build up in them, spreading even more allergens.

There is a way to reduce the particles that float in the air. A machine called a High Efficiency Particular Arrestance (HEPA) filter can actually remove floating particles from the air. These can be very helpful in sleeping areas.

Food Allergies

It might seem easy to avoid food-based allergens, but this is not always the case. One of the most troubling food allergies is to peanuts, which may affect as many as 1.5 million people in the United States alone. Peanut allergies are the leading cause of food-borne anaphylactic shock. Thousands of Americans require emergency medical treatment for peanut reactions every year. Unfortunately, as many as one hundred of these people die from the allergic reactions.

People who are highly sensitive to peanuts can have a reaction simply from touching a peanut or even a surface, such as a table, where peanuts have been lying. (This is why many school cafeterias now set aside "peanut-free" zones.) There

If you have a food allergy you must be very careful about reading labels. Most labels on packaged foods list their ingredients.

Sometimes people go too far in trying to "allergy-proof" their environment and these efforts can actually have the opposite effect. In the 1950s, many people who suffered from allergies began moving to the southwestern United States. They believed they would be healthier there, because many of the plants that caused their allergies were unknown in the desert landscape.

But the growth in population brought new housing, with lawns, shrubs, and trees and the allergens that come with them. Today, some parts of the Southwest actually have higher rates of allergies and asthma than the rest of the country. The city of Tucson, Arizona, now has four times as many cases of hay fever as the national average.

have even been reports of people suffering severe reactions on airplanes, when many people opened bags of nuts at once, releasing peanut dust into the air. Some airlines have stopped serving peanuts because of this problem.

Interestingly, there are some steps that can be taken to reduce the likelihood of food allergies appearing, especially in children. Pregnant women should eat only small amounts of certain foods that are known to contain allergens, such as eggs, milk, nuts, and shellfish. And very young children should probably avoid some of these foods—especially fish, shellfish, and peanutbutter—until they are at least two years old. Studies suggest that following these steps will help reduce the chance of a child having allergies later in life.

Another way to reduce allergic reactions to food is to avoid exercising for two hours after eating. Research has shown that exercise can sometimes trigger an allergic reaction.

Animal Dander

Nearly all of the common household pets can cause allergic reactions. Allergens may be in their hair, their skin, their feathers, even their saliva (spit), which can dry up and float through the air.

An allergist who discovers that someone is allergic to a household pet will almost always recommend removing

More than 60 percent of Americans live with at least one pet. Unfortunately, many of those pets cause allergic reactions in their owners.

the animal from the home. Of course, some people cannot bear to be separated from their pets. Those people should at least make sure that the animal does not sleep with them and that the floors and bedding are cleaned regularly to remove animal hair, skin, or saliva. These steps can be very helpful in reducing people's exposure to allergens.

ALLERGY TREATMENTS

Once an allergist has found the cause of a patient's allergies and ensured that everything possible has been done to reduce exposure to allergens, the next step is to find the correct treatment. There are several effective treatments that can reduce an allergy sufferer's sensitivity, or at least reduce the symptoms of an allergic reaction.

Antihistamines

Antihistamines block the effects of histamine, which causes swelling in the nose and other parts of the body. When taken during an allergic reaction, they can ease some of the most unpleasant allergy symptoms, including nasal congestion (stuffiness) and itching in the eyes. Antihistamines are available, with or without a doctor's prescription, in pills, nasal sprays, syrups, or eyedrops. But people who take antihistamines should be careful, because they can cause drowsiness or interact with other medication.

Decongestants

Decongestants shrink blood vessels, which reduces swelling in areas affected by allergies, such as the nose and eyes. Like antihistamines, they can be taken as pills, syrups, or nasal sprays during an allergic reaction. They are available with or without a prescription. But the side effects of decongestants are very

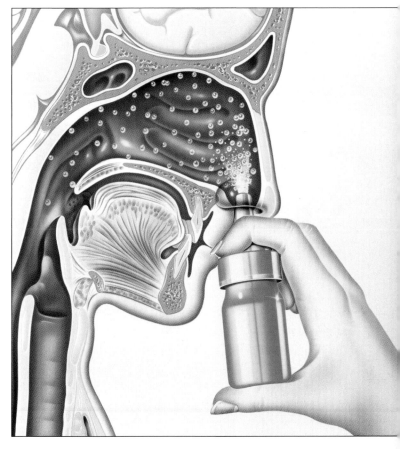

This illustration shows how a nasal spray works. The spray enters the tissue in the nose and in the airways, where it can be absorbed. Once it is absorbed, it starts preventing or lessening allergy symptoms.

different from those of antihistamines. They can cause sleeplessness and irritability. Decongestants can also be dangerous for people with certain medical problems, such as high blood pressure and an eye condition called glaucoma.

The Cost of Allergies

The National Institute of Allergy and Infectious Diseases estimates that every year, more than 50 million Americans suffer from allergy-related conditions. Allergies cause more than 16 million visits to doctors and other health care providers every year. Allergy-related conditions cost the nation's health care system more than $18 billion each year.

Corticosteroids

Unlike antihistamines and decongestants, this type of medication must be used regularly to be effective. Corticosteroids reduce swelling and inflammation in tissues, and are especially helpful with severe allergies and asthma. They can be taken in pill form, in inhalers, in nasal sprays, in creams— which are very helpful with skin allergies—and in eyedrops. However, they can cause serious side effects, especially for children, so they can only be used when prescribed by a doctor.

Bronchodilators

A bronchodilator is a type of medication, used in an inhaler, that can reduce the wheezing and shortness of breath caused by asthma. Bronchodilators work by loosening the muscles around the airways, and by removing mucus from the lungs.

They are available only by prescription, because they can cause serious medical problems, such as high blood pressure and a fast heartbeat.

Immunotherapy

Immunotherapy, or allergy shots, helps to prevent allergic reactions by reducing sensitivity to a particular allergen. The purpose of this therapy is to expose the person to the allergen in small doses until he or she gets used to the allergen and no long reacts to it. This treatment can be very effective against insect and pollen allergies, but does not seem to work well with most food allergies.

People with asthma use inhalers to help open their airways.

Allergy shots are a long-term treatment, and are always given under a doctor's care, after allergy tests have shown what substance is causing a reaction. In most cases, an allergy sufferer must have immunotherapy every ten days or so for almost a year to have good results. Some people may have to keep going back for as long as four years.

The allergy sufferer is given an injection in the arm. The injection contains a small amount of an allergen. The amount is increased slowly, over several weeks, while the doctor watches carefully for side effects. Because the injection contains an allergen, it can cause skin rash, itching, shortness of breath, and even—in rare cases—anaphylaxis.

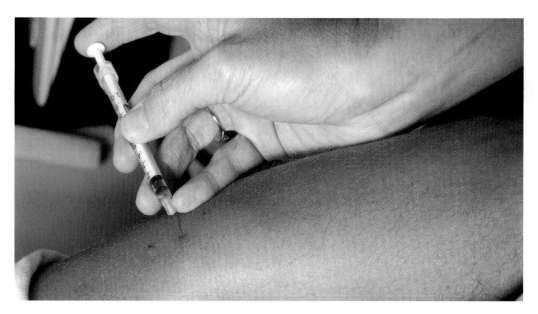

Immunotherapy is one of the best treatments for some types of allergies. But it can take years of repeated injections to be truly effective.

Emergency Medication

A doctor may prescribe an autoinjector (sometimes called an **epinephrine** pen) for people who have severe allergies. This is a small, pen-shaped device that has a needle that contains one dose of epinephrine. Epinephrine is a chemical used to stop allergic reactions. The autoinjector can be carried anywhere— to school, on the playground, even at the beach. This means that someone who has a severe allergic reaction can start treatment for the reaction immediately.

Someone who feels a severe allergic reaction beginning—for example, because of a bee sting—injects the medication into the soft tissue of the thigh. (The pen is designed so that a person can use it easily and quickly. He or she just removes the cap and pushes the pen into his or her leg.) The epinephrine quickly spreads, helping to prevent anaphylactic shock. But the medication wears off quickly, and it can also cause side effects, such as a fast heartbeat, dizziness, and nervousness. So someone who has used an autoinjector should seek medical care right away.

People keep their autoinjectors in their bags, in special carrying cases, or on straps around their necks.

There are many things we still do not understand about allergies. But doctors know more than ever before about what causes these mysterious reactions, and how to treat them. A true cure is probably many years away—but medical research is giving allergy sufferers hope that one day their sniffles, sneezes, and rashes will be a thing of the past.

GLOSSARY

allergen—A foreign substance in the body that causes an allergic reaction.

allergist—A doctor who specializes in diagnosing and treating allergies.

allergy—An extreme sensitivity to the presence of a foreign substance in the body.

anaphylaxis—An extreme, sometimes fatal, reaction to the presence of an antigen in the body.

antibiotic—A type of medicine that is used to fight infections caused by bacteria.

antibody—A substance (also called immunoglobulin) produced by the immune system in response to the presence of an antigen.

antigen—A foreign substance in the body that can cause disease or damage.

antihistamine—A type of allergy medicine that blocks the effects of histamine.

allergen—A substance that can cause an allergic reaction.

bacteria—A group of microorganisms (separate from viruses), many of which cause diseases.

dander—Material from animals (such as dog or cat hair or bird feathers) that can cause an allergic reaction.

dust mite—A microscopically small animal, related to spiders, that produces an allergen.

eczema—A skin condition that causes redness, itching, and sometimes blistering.

epinephrine—A drug that is used to treat asthma and extreme allergic reactions.

genetics—The study of how characteristics are passed on from parent to offspring (child).

hay fever—An allergy to pollen that causes sneezing, a stuffy nose, and itching eyes.

histamine—A chemical, released by the body during an allergic reaction, that causes swelling and inflammation.

hives—A blotchy rash or swelling of the skin (also called urticaria) caused by an allergic reaction.

immune system—The human body's defenses against attack by foreign substances, such as bacteria, viruses, and allergens.

immunity—The body's ability to resist the harmful effects of foreign substances.

immunotherapy—An allergy treatment that uses a weakened form of an allergen to reduce sensitivity to that allergen.

inflammation—Redness or swelling in a part of the body affected by an injury or a foreign substance.

latex—An extract from the sap of the rubber tree, used in many products, including tires, rubber gloves, and paint.

microorganism—A microscopically small living thing (such as a virus) that can often cause disease.

mold—A type of fungus.

pollen—Tiny grains, produced by flowering plants, weeds, and some trees, that help the plant reproduce.

rash—Redness or irritation of the skin.

respiratory system—The organs and airways that make breathing possible.

side effect—An unwanted reaction to a drug or some other type of medical treatment.

symptoms—Any changes in the body that signal the presence of an illness.

toxin—A poisonous substance produced by a living organism.

viruses—Microorganisms that cause many diseases in humans, animals, and plants.

FIND OUT MORE

Books

Brynie, Faith Hickman. *101 Questions About Your Immune System You Felt Defenseless to Answer...Until Now.* Brookfield, CT: Twenty-First Century Books, 2000.

Lipkowitz, Myron A. and Tova Navarra. *Encyclopedia of Allergies.* New York: Facts on File, 2001.

Moragne, Wendy. *Allergies.* Brookfield, CT: Twenty-First Century Books, 1999.

Peters, Celeste A. *Allergies, Asthma, and Exercise.* Austin, TX: Raintree Steck-Vaughn, 2000.

Silverstein, Alvin, Virginia Silverstein and Laura Silverstein Nunn. *Allergies.* Danbury, CT: Franklin Watts, 1999.

Web Sites

Asthma, Allergies, and Their Environmental Triggers
http://www.niehs.nih.gov/kids/asthma.htm

Asthma and Allergy Foundation of America
http://www.aafa.org/index.cfm

Food Allergy News for Kids
http://www.fankids.org/FANKid/kidindex.html

KidsHealth—Learning About Allergies
http://www.kidshealth.org/kid/asthma_basics/related/
  allergies.html

National Institute of Allergies and Infectious Diseases:
Allergy Statistics
http://www.niaid.nih.gov/factsheets/allergystat.htm

INDEX

Page numbers for illustrations are in **boldface**

ABOUT THE AUTHOR

Terry Allan Hicks has written books for Marshall Cavendish about subjects ranging from the common cold to the state of New Hampshire. He lives in Connecticut with his wife, Nancy, and their sons Jamie, Jack, and Andrew.